How to pay off your mortgage early

Forward

It's a pleasure to write this forward as the tips in this book to help you pay off your mortgage early will really help do just that.

I was lucky to be able to do just this about 5 years ago and the sense of financial freedom was amazing, so much so that just two years after we paid off our mortgage me wife and I moved to France.

A mortgage is without doubt the biggest debt a person will have in their lifetime, it can take a huge amount of a person's income to service this debt, imagine what you could do with that extra money?

I totally recommend this book and even if you only put into place a few of these tips you will see a reduction in the number of years you pay off your mortgage.

Good luck and see you on the other side of financial freedom

Darren Cox, living in France and living the dream.

How to pay off your mortgage early

We all want that bigger house with a nice kitchen and a bigger garden but have you ever wondered what you could do with all that money you shell out each month to pay for that dream place to live?

Many thousands of people will just go along with the banks recommendation of the set amount that is suggested they pay each month and the time scale dictated to them as well.

During the writing of this book we talked to a number of people about how they paid off their mortgage early and the difference it has made to their lives, some of their thoughts feature throughout the book.

You'd be amazed at the number of inventive and creative ways people have used to reduced their mortgage and we'll be going through some of them. However, the main connection between all of them was this one simple fact. They wanted financial freedom and knew that the only way of achieving this was to get rid of the largest debt they had.

Here's the scary bit, on a £200,000 (we are based in the UK but all these tips and ideas will work anywhere in the world) mortgage over 25 years you will end up paying around £321,900 that's over £120,000 you are paying to the bank for the privilege of borrowing money from them, wouldn't it be great to not give them all that money?

During the course of this book we will suggest lots of practical ways you can save money and put these savings towards paying off your mortgage earlier.

Dee and Stan

"We started doing car boot sales, we didn't make loads maybe £100 a month but you'd be amazed at what an

extra £1200 a year can make to the payment of your mortgage"

Let's give you a simple example of what could be achieved if you were to start paying a bit more each month.

If you have a £200'000 mortgage you will pay around £1000 a month for 25 years. If you were to pay an extra £100 per month you could reduce your mortgage by 3 years and 5 months and save you nearly £12,000.

If you could pay off an extra £5000 a year you'd reduce your mortgage by 9 years and save nearly £35,000, how amazing is that?

Don't take our word for it try out these links where you can add in some simple figures and work out for yourself how many years you could knock off your mortgage.

In the UK
www.moneysupermarket.com/mortgages/overpayment-calculator/

In the USA www.calculator.net/

Just type into a search engine in your country to find a payment calculator relevant to where you live.

We'll be giving examples of what you'll be saving throughout the book.

We should also point out though that we have no affiliate links or associations with any of the suggestions we share and do not receive payment from anyone.

Before we begin to show you how to pay off your mortgage early the first thing you need to find out is if you can actually pay more into your mortgage account than the monthly payments. You see the banks and lenders don't really want you to pay it off early because it means they don't make as much money, so they sell you mortgages that ties you in and doesn't allow for any flexibility.

Go to your lender and ask them, "Can we pay more and reduce our mortgage over time" if they say no, move your mortgage to one that will allow you too. You need to have the flexibility to be able to pay more as and when you can.

Also check that you won't be penalized for paying it off early, some lenders will slap on a fee at the end which can in some cases run into several thousand pounds.

Only change though if you are really serious about paying off your mortgage, as we've already said lenders don't want us to, so they may make you pay slightly more for a loan that allows you to do so. Check out the small print and if in doubt find an independent mortgage advisor to help you.

So how do you pay off your mortgage early and get that financial freedom you've been dreaming of?

There's a few ways to make this happen...

Make extra payments

There are a few ways you can make extra payments that will speed up the paying-off process.

The first way is to split your monthly mortgage payment in half and make bi-weekly payments instead. We know it sounds daft but by doing this, you'll end up making the equivalent of 13 months of mortgage payments instead of 12, an extra month's payment every year

Paying an extra £1000 a year will reduce your mortgage by 2 years 11 months and save you £10,500.

Again, you'll need to speak with your lender about whether they accept bi-weekly payments, some may not. In this case, it's up to you to set aside those bi-weekly payments.

Another approach is to pay more each month or a lump sum every couple of months to chip away at the loan faster, which can save you tens of thousands of pounds over the life of your loan.

We've already given you one example but let's put that into practical terms.

How many of you pop out from work at lunchtime and buy a sandwich, drink and a chocolate bar? Quite a few we would expect. You can very easily spend £10 a day, times that by 20 days and you spend at least £200 a month. if you were to make these payments into your mortgage account and make your own sandwiches you could knock off 5 years and 10 months form your mortgage and save a staggering £20,572 pounds!

Just by stopping buying that coffee on the way to the office you'd be adding £100 a month to your mortgage repayment and we already know how much that saves you.

It's the little things that will make a difference and will be less noticeable to your life.

We go into more details later regarding ways to save money and repay your mortgage quicker.

However again If you go this route make sure to check with your lender that the payments will be applied in the correct way to reduce the loan and not the interest. You'll also want to make sure they understand the extra payment is not for the next month's mortgage payment but an additional payment.

Sue and Pete, Wimbledon, London

"We decided we wanted to pay off our mortgage early and from then on we did want ever we could make it happen, it became a bit of a competition between us to see who had saved the most each month"

Refinance your mortgage

Refinancing or change your mortgage to pay it off early only makes sense if you can get a lower interest rate. Keep in mind, there are fees associated with refinancing or changing so you want to make sure the savings cancels out the cost of moving it.

Refinancing into a shorter-term loan, such as going from a 25-year mortgage to a 20-year mortgage, puts you on the path to early payoff. Use a mortgage calculator to compare payments and total interest saved between a 25-year and 20-year term, obviously you'll be paying a bit more each month but sometimes people like the structure of regular payments rather than paying extra as and when you have it.

Make lump sum payments toward your loan

An alternative to refinancing is to make lump-sum payments to your loan when you can. Homeowners who get large bonuses or those who inherit money or sell valuable items, might choose to use the extra cash to pay down the loan.

With some mortgage providers, you must specify when extra money is to be put toward the loan. Once again check with your loan provider if you are unsure how additional payments will affect your mortgage.

One off lump sums don't always look great in the overall scheme of repayments of your mortgage, an example of just paying a lump sum once of £10,000 only reduces your mortgage by 1 year 9 months and saves you £9950 over the life of the mortgage.

Steve and Tony

"We decided we wanted to travel more but knew we couldn't whilst we had a large mortgage, we set out with the goal of paying it off as quickly as we could and were amazed when we did it in 5 years, we never thought we could"

Going down the saving money route

So, there you are it sounds simple, doesn't it? Only joking, of course it isn't, it'll be a long process and will take dedication.

However, it's worth it, can you imagine having that financial freedom and the extra money every single month?

So, you next need to decide if you want to do it, are you in it for the long haul, the nights not going out if you decide to save? if you think you do then you need to find out if you can Pay Off My Mortgage Early?

Check with your mortgage company first. Some companies only accept extra payments at specific times or may charge prepayment penalties.

Always Include a note on your extra payment that you want it applied to the principal balance—not to the following month's payment.

Once you've made sure you can make extra payments you need to have a plan.

Set yourself goals, a timescale and spending plan, you're much more likely to change your spending habits if you're saving with something specific in mind. How many times have you wanted that new outfit or latest gadget and decided to save for it, well paying off your mortgage is just like saving for that new outfit, just a very expensive outfit!

All we're trying to say is think of something you want to do once you've paid off your mortgage and pin a picture of that goal onto your fridge, it'll help during the hard times and focus your mind.

Ok we know it's a long-term goal so break it down, maybe into 1 year, 5 years and 10 years plans. Set a goal that will let you achieve these short-term goals, such as "We want to pay off at least £25,000 more in five years". You can mentally prepare for what will be more of a savings marathon, if your focus is on smaller short-term goals.

No matter how big your target is, you first of all need to see where all of your money is going before you can figure out how much you'll be able to save and add towards your overall extra payments be that monthly, quarterly or yearly. The easiest way to do this is on the first day of next month, look at what you spent the previous month, putting essentials and non-essentials into two lists. Also carry a little note pad with you and write down every time you take money out the bank, pay cash for something etc. You'd be amazed how those little £1 here £1 there soon mount up over a month!

Essentials and non-essentials

Essentials are the fixed costs that you need to pay, such as your existing mortgage, any loans, car repayments, food shop, utilities etc. these have some flexibility but not as much as Non-essentials where you more room for movement, for example, take aways, nights out, bottle of wine with the meal at home and those lunches and coffee you get whilst at work. These all mount up.

If you have a bottle of wine with your meal 2 or 3 times a week at say £5 a bottle that adds up to nearly £800 a year, include those £10 meals every day and cut down on those Indian take away by one a week and it could add up too nearly £800 every single month. And here's the staggering bit you could knock off 13 years and 8 months from your mortgage and save over £46000 from the repayments!

Ok but you're now thinking "yer but isn't life during those other 12 years gonna be boring and we're going lose all our friends as we never go out" True so you need to find a happy medium.

Stuart and Mary

"We told our friends what we were doing and were amazed that 2 of them wanted to join us on the journey and do the same thing, we would share tips on things we saved money on, eventually all our friends went on the journey with us"

Consider what you could forego without becoming "billy no mates" and commit to putting that money away. For example, could you skip takeout's three times a week down to twice a week and cook at home instead, that would save you £1300 a year? What about eating out? If you're spending £200 a month at restaurants, could you look at a way to shave £50 of your monthly eating out bill, this would save you £600 a year. Just these two adjustments could still knock off 4 years and 11 moths from your mortgage and save you nearly £18000.

So, what's the actual figure you should be saving?

Well anything between 10% to 20% of your income each month is a good benchmark. You Could adopt the 50-30-20 rule, which is 50% of your take-home pay goes toward essentials, 30% goes toward non-essentials and 20% goes toward savings and it's this 20% area where you make your money to pay off your mortgage.

For just one month list everything you spend, even the little things, a newspaper on the way to work or the app you spend 99p on every month, list everything. You will be shocked first of all how much goes out without you realizing and then you'll be more determined to beat the banks and keep some of your hard-earned money.

Donna and Ian

"We used to spend a lot on cable TV and realized we never watched a lot of the channels we actually paid for, we stopped all of them saving us over £70 a month"

So here are some tips to help you.

Do it together

If you have a partner you really need to decide if this is something you both want to do, saving money isn't always easy, sharing the progress and seeing your mortgage go down is great. We mentioned Sue and Pete earlier that have competitions to see who can save the most over the month, whoever wins gets to spend £50 on whatever they want, and you know what usually happens? That £50 also goes into the saving pot.

Get Rid of High-Interest Debt

Credit card bills are without doubt the worse culprit when it comes to high interest payments and is the first thing you should tackle if you are serious about paying off your mortgage early.

One option, if you have a few cards and pay a high amount each month paying them off is to roll them all into one loan and then cut up the cards. A bank loan is going to give you a lower interest rate to pay than a credit card and it'll be paid off as the bank will take it automatically instead of just paying the minimum amount each month on the credit card debt. Once that loan is paid off, you can put the amount you were paying each month into savings instead.

Make saving Automatic

Every month, schedule an amount of money to be transferred regularly into a savings account. This reduces the risk of you spending the money before it's saved. Putting £100 each month into a savings account and then at the end of each year paying that lump sum off your mortgage will mean a reduction of 3 years and 5 months and a saving of just over £12000

Save any "gift money"

If you're like us we have relatives that don't know what to buy us for birthdays and Christmas. Tell them what you are doing and ask for money instead of a gift you might never use.

Every little bit you can save and use to pay off your mortgage will work towards that goal.

Go through all your utilities

It's easy to just set up a direct debit for your phone, insurance, electric and other utilities and then just let then continue year after year, however check that you are getting the best service and price, you'd be amazed how much you could save. Also do you need a landline and a mobile now days? You'll probably need a line coming into your house for internet but do you also need a line to make calls, probably not, most mobile providers now have plans that give you free calls to mobile or other landlines, check this out and work out what's your best option.

Wait

We all get tempted to buy the latest gadget and can't wait to get online to buy it, but try the 3-day rule. Avoid impulse buys, Impose the 3-day rule and see if you still want that item, chances are you won't and you've saved yourself some more money that you should put away into your saving pot.

Kate and Paul

"We decided to see if we could grocery shop for the two of us for just £50 a week, the first few times it was hard but after a while it got easier, we still blow out a few times and spend a bit more but the money we saved has really helped towards paying off our mortgage."

So, you've gone through your monthly outgoings and can't find a way to save anything let us help, here's a few quick tips that might help you on your way.

1. **Cut your own hair.** Ok this is easier for men, get a good hair razor and your away. **savings (depending where you go) £10 a month**.
2. **Fill your name brand cereal box with the supermarkets own brand.** In fact, not just cereal, did you know that the majority of store brands are actually made for them by the brand and just repackaged into the stores own boxes, don't believe us well just type ito Google "store brands vs name brands" and see for yourself. **Savings £600 a year**
3. **Buy a water filter and then fill up from home.** Do you buy a bottle of water going to work, at the gym why? Buy a water filter and fill up at your own tap every day, n1ot only will you be

saving a load of money but you'll also won't be buying non-recyclable plastic. **Saving £730 a year**

4. **Bring your lunch to work.** We've touched on this earlier but it's a huge saving. **Saving £2400 a year**

5. **Stop paying for TV**. The average monthly cable bill is over £75. Including Sky, Netflix, Amazon Prime to name just a few. Ok we'll ease you down gently cut down on one. **Saving £300 a year**

6. Plan your meals better. How often do you run into the local shop to pick up something to cook that evening, we know we all lead busy lives but planning your meals for the coming week could save you loads. **Saving £260 a year.**

7. When you were a kid did you have a jar that you'd put all the small change into? Some of us used too and we've all said how amazed we used to be when we emptied it and how much money was in there. Go back to being a kid again and start a jar with your small change.

8. Ok we don't want to preach here but if you smoke not only would it be a good idea to stop but have you actually worked out how much you spend? A pack of 20 is around £9, if you smoke 1 pack a day that's £3285 a year! **Saving 7 years 7 months and £26,700**

Just doing these 8 things would save you a staggering £31,110 every year and you'd pay off your mortgage in just over 5 years.

There's other options rather than saving, you could earn more. Do you have time for a 2nd job? Could you do a passive income, we are great fans of this way here at business with Joe, check out our other books where we go into a lot more detail on how to make passive incomes but here's just a quick overview

Passive income is when you make something once but it sells over and over again, this book is a prime example of a passive income but there are lots of other examples.

Finding a passive income idea is great because you can focus on other things whilst you continue to earn a great income.

Now, you need to do something in the beginning to start earning passive income. That work can be either a time or financial investment. But, after most of the leg work is done, income continually comes in without much effort from you. This makes it one of the best ways to save money for years to come.

Various passive income ideas include:

- Affiliate marketing
- High yield savings accounts
- Rental real estate
- Rent out a room in your home
- Sell your photo's
- Blogging
- Writing a book
- Starting an online store
- Creating an online course

The other option for earning money is with an active income, with an active income you basically get paid for the time you put in.

Could you work in a bar or a restaurant a few nights a week? How about teaching online? Do you have a skill and could you sell it on Fiverr? There are lots of ways to earn but you need to think long and hard about active incomes as a way of paying off your mortgage, it'll take time.

An example, if you worked two night a week in a bar and earning £100, you worked 35 weeks that's £3500 a year you'd save nearly 8 years off your mortgage but it would still mean working for 17 years in the bar.

Bob and Sonja

"We tried all sorts of things, taking on extra work but in the end we just cut back and paid off our mortgage early like that."

We suggest you download a budgeting app and set yourself a monthly goal, seeing things written down and watching your saving go up and less money going out is so much more fun than working it all out on bits of paper.

Finally

Hundreds of people pay off their mortgage early and they all had one thing in common, they started! Sounds easy doesn't it but you'd be amazed at the number of people we've talked too that say, "we'd love to pay off our mortgage" and then when you see them a year later they still haven't started, they are still paying loads of money to the bank or loan provider.

Even if you decide to look into the possibility, ask your bank if you can, work out ways of making savings at least you are doing more than most.

Taking that first step will see you on the road to financial freedom and potentially a new life.

Go on what have you got to lose?

You can have results or excuses but you can't have both

Stay connected on:

Facebook - /businesswithjoe

Twitter – @BusinessWithJo1

Instagram - business_with_joe

YouTube – search - business with Joe

Our website – www.businesswithjoe.com